A Guide for Using

The Black Pearl

in the Classroom

Based on the book written by Scott O'Dell

Written by Concetta Doti Ryan

Illustrated by Keith Vasconcelles

Teacher Created Resources, Inc.
6421 Industry Way
Westminster, CA 92683
www.teachercreated.com

ISBN: 978-1-55734-410-6

©1992 Teacher Created Resources, Inc.
Reprinted, 2012
Printed in U.S.A.

Table of Contents

Introduction

A good book can touch our lives like a good friend. Within its pages are words and characters that can inspire us to achieve our highest ideals. We can turn to it for companionship, recreation, comfort, and guidance. It also gives us a cherished story to hold in our hearts forever.

In Literature Units, great care has been taken to select books that are sure to become good friends!

Teachers who use this literature unit will find the following features to supplement their own valuable ideas.

- Sample Lesson Plans

- Pre-reading Activities

- A Biographical Sketch and Picture of the Author

- A Book Summary

- Vocabulary Lists and Suggested Vocabulary Activities

- Chapters grouped for study, with each section including:

  — *quizzes*

  — *hands-on projects*

  — *cooperative learning activities*

  — *cross-curriculum connections*

  — *extensions into the reader's own life*

- Post-reading Activities

- Book Report Ideas

- Research Ideas

- A Culminating Activity

- Three Different Options for Unit Tests

- Bibliography

- Answer Key

We are confident that this unit will be a valuable addition to your planning, and hope that as you use our ideas, your students will increase the circle of "friends" that they can have in books!

Sample Lesson Plan

Each of the lessons suggested below can take from one to several days to complete.

LESSON 1

- Introduce and complete some or all of the pre-reading activities found on page 5.
- Read "About the Author" with your students. (page 6)
- Introduce vocabulary list for SECTION 1. (page 8) Ask students for possible definitions.

LESSON 2

- Read Chapters 1 through 4. Place vocabulary words in context and discuss their meanings.
- Choose a vocabulary activity. (page 9)
- Discuss scuba diving techniques. (page 12)
- Complete character sketches. (page 13)
- Discuss the geographical setting of the story. (page 14)
- Begin "Reading Response Journals." (page 15)
- Administer the SECTION 1 quiz. (page 11)
- Introduce the vocabulary list for SECTION 2. (page 8) Ask students for possible definitions.

LESSON 3

- Read Chapters 5 through 1O. Place vocabulary words in context and discuss their meanings.
- Choose a vocabulary activity. (page 9)
- Write newspaper articles. (page 17)
- Hold a mock auction. (page 18)
- Discuss the book in terms of math. (page 19)
- Choose an ecology project. (page 20)
- Discuss legends and superstitions. (page 21)
- Administer SECTION 2 quiz. (page 16)
- Introduce the vocabulary list for SECTION 3. (page 8) Ask students for possible definitions.

LESSON 4

- Read Chapters 11 through 13. Place vocabulary words in context and discuss their meanings.
- Choose a vocabulary activity. (page 9)
- Design a wanted poster. (page 23)

- Introduce figurative language. (page 24)
- Discuss the book in terms of science. (page 25)
- Discuss moral dilemmas. (page 26)
- Administer SECTION 3 quiz. (page 22)
- Introduce vocabulary list for SECTION 4. (page 8) Ask students for possible definitions.

LESSON 5

- Read Chapters 14 through 18. Place vocabulary words in context and discuss their meanings.
- Choose a vocabulary activity. (page 9)
- Make a storyboard. (page 28)
- Rewrite the ending. (page 29)
- Discover other marine life. (pages 30-31)
- Discuss the book in terms of art. (page 32)
- Discuss the missing children crisis. (page 33)
- Administer SECTION 4 quiz. (page 27)
- Assign the word search. (page 34)

LESSON 6

- Discuss any questions your students may have about the book. (page 35)
- Assign book reports and research projects. (pages 36 and 37)
- Begin work on culminating activity. (pages 38, 39, 40, and 41)
- Assign the crossword puzzle. (page 10)

LESSON 7

- Complete and present culminating activity.
- Administer unit tests: 1, 2, and/or 3. (pages 42, 43, and 44)
- Discuss the test answers and other possibilities.
- Discuss the students' enjoyment of the book.
- Provide a list of related reading for your students. (page 45)

Before the Book

Build background knowledge by introducing the following information to students.

An old Arab legend tells us that pearls were formed when dew drops filled with moonlight fell into the ocean and were swallowed by oysters. The modern scientific explanation is not nearly as romantic, but still quite fascinating. A natural pearl (often called an Oriental pearl) forms when an irritant works its way into a particular species of oyster, mussel, or clam. As a defense mechanism, the mollusk secretes a fluid to coat the irritant. Layer upon layer of this coating is deposited on the irritant until a lustrous pearl is formed.

A cultured pearl undergoes the same process. The only difference is that the irritant is a surgically-implanted mother-of-pearl bead or piece of shell. The core is therefore much larger than in a natural pearl. However, the size of the nucleus does not matter.

Fine pearl waters are quite rare. The Persian Gulf has always been the source of the finest saltwater pearls. Other sources include: Mexico, Japan, Australia, Panama, and Venezuela.

Before you begin reading *The Black Pearl* with your students, do some pre-reading activities to stimulate interest and enhance comprehension. Here are some activities that might work well in your class.

1. Predict what the story might be about by hearing the title.

2. Predict what the story might be about by looking at the cover illustration.

3. Discuss other books by Scott O'Dell that students may have heard about or read. (Examples: *Island of the Blue Dolphins, Sing Down the Moon, Sarah Bishop, Carlota, My Name is Not Angelica*)

4. Answer these questions:
   Are you interested in:
   — a story about a young boy who becomes a hero?
   — a story about diving in the sea?
   — a story about finding something of great value?

5. Work in groups to create your own underwater adventure story. Present the story to the class as a narration, or dramatize it, adding props and scenery.

6. Use the picture on page 48 to help introduce *The Black Pearl* to your class. The picture can also be used as a journal cover or the centerpiece of a bulletin board display of student work.

About the Author

Scott O'Dell was born and raised in Los Angeles, California. As a child, his family moved around quite a bit. Scott O'Dell has lived in San Pedro, which is part of Los Angeles, and Rattlesnake Island, which is across the bay from San Pedro. He also lived in Claremont, which is just east of Los Angeles, and Julian, an old gold mining town. Scott O'Dell said that growing up in these rich settings helped to give his books the sound of the sea and the feel of the frontier.

Mr. O'Dell was educated at Occidental College, the University of Wisconsin, Stanford University, and the University of Rome. After college, he was a cameraman on the second company of the original motion picture of *Ben Hur*. He was with the air force in Texas during World War II and then became a book editor for a Los Angeles newspaper.

Mr. O'Dell's love for history shows in the many historical novels he has written. He chose these generally because he felt that children need to know and understand the past. On this issue he comments:

> *"For children, who believe that nothing much has happened before they appeared and that what little of the past they do perceive has any possible bearing upon their lives, the historical novel can be an entertaining corrective, a signpost between the fixed, always relevant, past and the changing present."*

Scott O'Dell won the Newbery Medal in 1961 for his classic story *Island of the Blue Dolphins*. He is a three time Newbery Honor Book winner. The honor books include: *The Black Pearl, Sing Down the Moon,* and *The King's Fifth.* In addition to these awards, he is the winner of the deGrummond and Regina Medals and is the recipient of the Hans Christian Anderson Author Medal. This medal, which Scott O'Dell won in 1972, is the highest international recognition for a body of work by an author of children's books.

> *"Writing for children is more fun than writing for adults and more rewarding. Children have the ability, which most adults have lost, the knack to be someone else, of living through stories the lives of other people. Six months after publication of an adult book there's a big silence. But with a book for children it's just the opposite. If children like your book they respond for a long time, by thousands of letters. It is this response, this concern and act of friendship, that for me makes the task of writing worth doing."*

*(Quotations from **Something About the Author**. Ed. Anne Commire. Gale Research Company)*

The Black Pearl

by Scott O'Dell

Dell, 1967

Available in Canada from Thomas Allen & Son

Ramon Salazar is a 16-year-old boy living in La Paz, Mexico. He has recently been made a partner in his father's pearl business. However, as Ramon works in the office of Salazar and Son he longs to be out in the Vermilion Sea, diving for pearls with his father and the others. Unfortunately, Ramon's father feels that he is better suited for office work.

Ramon, desperate to learn to dive for pearls, solicits the help of a local Indian named Luzon. Luzon teaches Ramon how to dive, and in return Ramon agrees to pay Luzon for the pearls that he finds in Luzon's lagoon. Little did either of them know that Ramon would find a 62.3 carat black pearl.

Ramon and his father agree to sell the pearl. However, when they are not offered what they feel the pearl is worth, they hastily decide to donate the pearl to the church. The priest assures them that because of their generosity they will surely be favored in Heaven. Luzon, on the other hand, warns them of the danger they are in because the great pearl belongs to the Manta Diablo, or monster devilfish.

After the storm destroys Ramon's father's fleet and claims the lives of his father and the other divers, Ramon decides that he must return the pearl to the Manta Diablo. After stealing the pearl from the church, Ramon begins his voyage back to the lagoon where he originally found the pearl. However, Sevillano, a greedy diver from Ramon's father's fleet, follows Ramon to the lagoon. Ramon is surprised to see Sevillano because he didn't believe anyone from the fleet survived the storm. Sevillano wants the pearl in order to sell it himself. So, he forces Ramon to head back toward La Paz.

On their way back to La Paz, the Manta Diablo begins following their boat. Ramon fears for his life. Sevillano, angered by the presence of the Manta Diablo, decides to kill it. However, as Sevillano thrusts the deadly harpoon into the Manta Diablo he suddenly gets tangled in the rope and drowns.

With the Manta Diablo and Sevillano both dead, Ramon heads back to La Paz. Upon his return, he anonymously returns the pearl to the church where it belongs.

Vocabulary

On this page are vocabulary lists which correspond to each sectional grouping of chapters. Vocabulary activity ideas can be found on page 9 of this book. Vocabulary knowledge may be evaluated by including selected words in the quizzes and tests. This can be done with multiple choice, matching, or fill-in-the-blank questions.

SECTION 1
(Chapters 1-4)

ambergris	sickle
puny	gilt
ledger	shrewd
carat	braggart
prow	stern
timid	vermillion
niche	tentacle
benediction	astern
headland	

SECTION 2
(Chapters 5-10)

lagoon	fathom
channel	pinnacle
gleam	serpent
throng	seize
flaw	paragon
calipers	glisten
flourish	niche
incense	prosper

SECTION 3
(Chapters 11-13)

resent	strewn
overcast	huddle
mourners	scoff
belfry	admonition
desperation	gunwale
avail	provisions
sombrero	mackerel

SECTION 4
(Chapters 14-18)

tiller	rudder
furlong	malice
barren	disgust
manhood	betray
thrust	grunt
taut	adversary
adoration	slacken

SPANISH WORDS

Manta Diablo—monster devilfish *fiesta*—party
siesta—afternoon nap
chubasco—very strong wind
calabozo—jail
coromuel—light wind
frijoles—beans

Vocabulary Activity Ideas

You can help your students learn and retain the vocabulary in *The Black Pearl* by providing them with interesting vocabulary activities. Here are a few ideas to try.

❑ Challenge your students to a **Vocabulary Bee!** This is similar to a spelling bee, but in addition to spelling each word correctly, the game participants must correctly define the words as well.

❑ As a group activity, have students work together to create an **Illustrated Dictionary** of the vocabulary words.

❑ Play **20 Clues** with the entire class. In this game, one student selects a vocabulary word and gives clues about this word, one by one, until someone in the class can guess the word.

❑ Play **Vocabulary Charades**. In this game, vocabulary words are acted out.

❑ Encourage students to keep a **Vocabulary Journal** where they can list words they are unfamiliar with, but did not appear on the vocabulary list.

❑ Have students locate the vocabulary word in the story. Then proceed to have them guess the meaning by using **Context Clues**.

❑ Challenge students to find **Synonyms or Antonyms** for the vocabulary words from within the story.

❑ Play **Vocabulary Concentration**. The goal of this game is to match vocabulary words with their definitions. Divide the class into groups of 2-5 students. Have the students make two sets of cards the same size and color. On one set have them write the vocabulary words. On the second set have them write the definitions. All cards are mixed together and placed face down on the table. A player picks two cards. If the pair matches the word with its definition, the player keeps the cards and takes another turn. If the cards don't match, they are returned to their places face down on the table, and another player takes a turn. Players must concentrate to remember the locations of the words and their definitions. The game continues until all matches have been made. This is an ideal activity for free exploration time.

❑ Have students complete the **Crossword Puzzle** and **Word Search** contained in this unit. The puzzle may be done as a culminating activity or vocabulary pre-test.

❑ Challenge your students to use a specific vocabulary word from the story at least **10 Times In One Day**. They must keep a record of when, how, and why the word was used!

You probably have more ideas to add to this list. Try them. See if experiencing vocabulary on a personal level increases your students' vocabulary interest and retention.

Crossword Puzzle

Across

5. semicircle shape
6. one who boasts
7. to take legal possession of
8. a lever used to steer a boat
9. fearful
10. a model of perfection
11. recklessness because of despair
17. tightly stretched
18. ones who express sorrow
19. lacking vegetation
21. a unit for measuring distance
23. a flat movable piece hinged to the rear of a ship for steering

Down

1. desire to harm others
2. an imperfection
3. to shine by reflected light
4. a unit of length equal to six feet
5. rear part of a boat
9. to push with sudden force
12. a shallow body of water
13. an enemy
15. to mock
16. to feel strongly against
20. behind a ship or aircraft
22. gold leaf or color

Quiz Time!

1. On the back of this paper, write a one paragraph summary of the major events in each chapter of this section. Then complete the rest of the questions on this page.

2. Ramon describes the Manta Diablo as the most beautiful creature he has ever seen. Yet, it is also evil. How can something be both beautiful and evil?

   _____

   _____

3. Why doesn't Ramon's father want Ramon to sail with the fleet?

   _____

4. Why doesn't Ramon's father want people to think of Ramon as puny?

   _____

5. Who is sailing on the *Santa Theresa*?

   _____

6. What type of person is Gaspar Ruiz? What does he look like?

   _____

   _____

7. Ramon's father warns Ramon to stay away from Ruiz because he is a trouble maker. If this is true, why does Ramon's father allow Ruiz to sail with them?

   _____

   _____

8. Why does Ramon offer to pay Luzon for pearls that he finds in the lagoon?

   _____

   _____

9. What is Ramon's dream?

   _____

   _____

   _____

10. On the back of this paper, draw what the Manta Diablo looks like.

Scuba Diving: Past and Present

The diving equipment used by Ramon and the other divers in *The Black Pearl* differs greatly from the type of scuba equipment used today. Look at the two pictures below. First, label the equipment in pictures A and B. Then, answer the questions that follow.

Picture A

Label the picture using these words: fins, snorkel, dive timer, knife, compass, wet suit, depth gauge, mask, cylinder of compressed air, mouthpiece, weight belt, and life jacket.

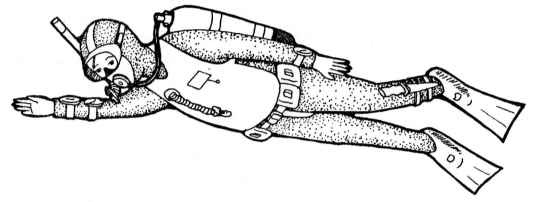

Picture B

Label the picture using these words: sink stone, knife, and rope.

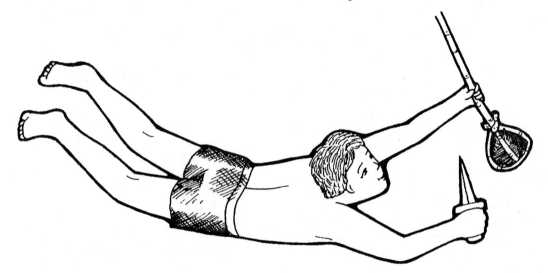

1. How does the equipment we use today differ from that used by Ramon and the other divers?

   _____

2. Choose three items from the equipment listed in picture A and research what they are used for and how. Present your findings to the class.

3. When Ramon was learning how to dive, air tanks hadn't been invented yet. Divers could only stay underwater as long as they could hold their breath. Sevillano claimed to be able to hold his breath for four minutes. Using a timer, find out and report how long you can hold your breath.

Character Sketches

Ramon and Sevillano are two main characters in the story. In this activity, you will complete the chart below by comparing and contrasting Ramon and Sevillano. When comparing characters, you explain how they are alike. When you contrast characters, you explain how they are different.

Complete the chart by listing details about the personalities of the two main characters.

Personality Chart	
Ramon	**Sevillano**

Using the list generated above, underline the ways in which the two characters are alike. Look at the diagram below. This is known as a Venn diagram. Notice that there are two circles, each containing the name of one of the main characters. Next, notice how the two circles overlap. Using the information generated in the chart above, it is easy to complete the Venn diagram. In the outer edges of the circles, list the characteristics that the characters DO NOT have in common. Within the center portion, where the two circles overlap, list the ways in which the characters are alike. Be prepared to discuss whether Ramon and Sevillano are more alike or different.

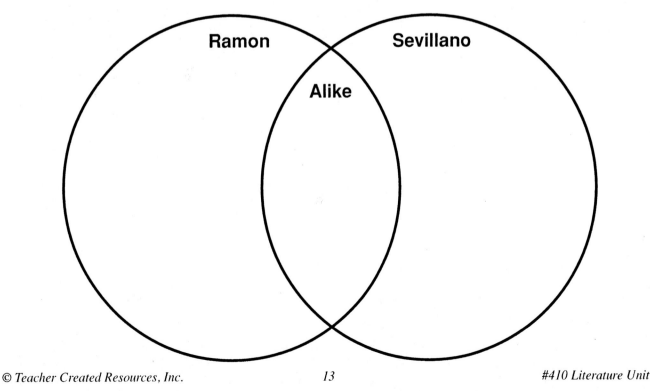

Geography

It is important to know the setting of any story that you read. The setting of *The Black Pearl* is La Paz, Mexico. Locate La Paz on a classroom map if one is available. Then locate La Paz on the map to the right. Also, locate these other cities mentioned in the story: Mazatlan, Mexico City, and Guadalajara.

Considering its location, why do you think La Paz is a good place to dive for pearls?

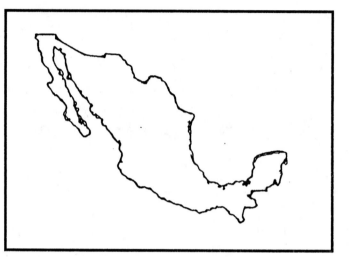

_____

_____

There are few countries in the world that have fine pearl waters such as Mexico. The Persian Gulf has always been the source of the finest saltwater pearls. Other sources include: Australia, Japan, Panama, and Venezuela. Locate each of these places on the world map below and then answer the question at the bottom of the page.

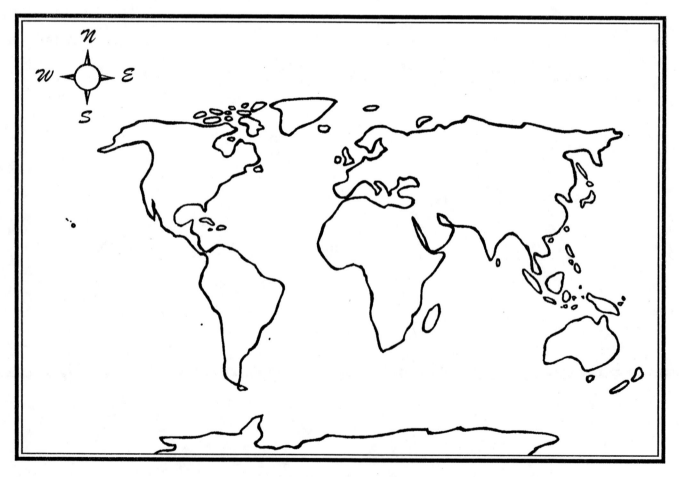

What do you think each of these pearling regions have in common?

_____

Reading Response Journals

One great way to insure that the reading of *The Black Pearl* touches every student in a personal way is to include the use of Reading Response Journals in your plans. In these journals, students can be encouraged to respond to the story in a number of ways. Here are a few ideas.

- Tell students the purpose of the journal is to record their thoughts, ideas, observations, and question as they read *The Black Pearl*.

- Provide students with, or ask them to suggest, topics from the story that would stimulate writing. Here are a few examples from the chapters in SECTION 1.

  — List some ways in which Ramon's responsibilities differ from those of a sixteen year old living in the United States today.

  — Describe the type of person Sevillano is. Do you think he has many friends? Would you like to be his friend? Why or why not?

  — How do you think Ramon's father will react when he finds out that Ramon is taking diving lessons? Do you think it was wrong for Ramon to take lessons without permission?

- After the reading of each chapter, students can write one or more new things they learned in the chapter.

- Ask students to draw their responses to certain events or characters in the story, using the blank pages in their journals.

- Tell students they may use their journals to record "diary-type" responses that they may want to enter.

- Encourage students to bring their journal ideas to life! Ideas generated from their journal writing can be used to create plays, debates, stories, songs, and art displays.

Allow students time to write in their journals daily. To evaluate the journals, you may wish to use the following guidelines.

- Personal reflections will be read by the teacher, but no corrections or letter grades will be assigned. Credit is given for effort, and all students who sincerely try will be awarded credit. If a grade is desired for this type of entry, grade according to the number of journal entries completed. For example, if five journal assignments were made and the student conscientiously completes all five, then he or she should receive an "A."

- Non-judgmental teacher responses should be made as you read the journals to let the students know that you are reading and enjoying their journals. Here are some types of responses that will please your journal writers and encourage them to write more.

  — "You have really found what's important in the story!"

  — "You write so clearly I almost feel as if I'm there."

  — "If you feel comfortable, I'd like for you to share this with the class."

Quiz Time!

1. On the back of this paper, write a one paragraph summary of the major events in each chapter of this section. Then complete the rest of the questions on this page.

2. How does Luzon know when the Manta Diablo is in the lagoon?

   _____

3. Ramon said the lagoon made him feel "uneasy." What do you think he meant by this?

   _____

   _____

4. Why hasn't Luzon ever searched for pearls in the cave of his lagoon?

   _____

   _____

5. How much does the great pearl weigh?

   _____

6. Why does Ramon deny finding the pearl?

   _____

   _____

7. Why doesn't Luzon want to help Ramon pry open the giant shell?

   _____

8. Why do the pearl dealers criticize the pearl and then offer to buy it?

   _____

   _____

9. How does Ramon's family react to the father's decision to donate the pearl to the church?

   _____

   _____

10. Think about what Ramon did after he found the pearl. How might Sevillano have acted in the same situation? Write your answer on the back of this page.

News Flash!

Pretend that you are a newspaper reporter for a local newspaper in La Paz. Write a front page story announcing the finding of the great pearl. You may include community comments and quotes from Ramon (what you think he may have said). Draw a picture and caption in the box to go along with the story and add your own headline.

Volume 1   Date:

Title

by

Best Buys!

In chapter nine of *The Black Pearl,* Ramon and his father try to sell the Great Pearl of Heaven to some local pearl dealers. They begin the exchange by setting their price at 20,000 pesos. The pearl dealers feel this price is too high, and so they offer 10,000 pesos. Ramon's father insists that he will not take less than 20,000 pesos for the pearl. The dealers raise their offer several more times. Their final offer is 15,000 pesos. The exchange that took place between Ramon's father and the dealers is sometimes referred to as "haggling" over a price.

Hold a dass auction. Divide into groups with each group of students receiving a set amount of money to spend. With this money your group can bid on items that the class brings to "sell." Prepare for the auction by completing the worksheet below.

Item	Asking Price (Minimum Bid)	Actual Amount Received

Money! Money! Money!

Locate information about current exchange rates. The newspaper and travel magazines are possible sources for this data. Using a calculator, answer the questions below.

1. Ramon's father is asking 20,000 pesos for the great pearl. How much is this in United States dollars?

   _____

2. Initially the pearl dealers offer 10,000 pesos for the pearl. How much is this?

   _____

3. Convert these other offers into United States money.

   11,000 pesos _____   13,250 pesos _____

   12,000 pesos _____   15,000 pesos _____

   12,250 pesos _____   25,000 pesos _____

4. Each type of currency has a different exchange rate. Convert the following amounts into United States dollars.

   20,000 lire _____ *(Italy)*

   20,000 yen _____ *(Japan)*

   20,000 drachmas _____ *(Greece)*

   20,000 pounds _____ *(Britain)*

   20,000 francs _____ *(France)*

   20,000 deutschemarks _____ *(Germany)*

Ecologically Speaking...

The setting for *The Black Pearl* centers around Baja, California. The sea played a vital role in the lives of the people of La Paz.

Today many of our beaches and waterways are becoming polluted due to human carelessness, indifference, and ignorance. Some things, such as oil spills, are not the direct results of your actions. However, there are positive steps that you can take to prevent any more litter on the shores, as well as pollution, poisoning, and entanglement in the ocean.

Activity: Choose one or more of the sample projects listed below. Put a check in the box(es) for the project(s) you have chosen. Write an account or give an oral report to the class when you have completed your project.

❏ When you are at the beach, take along a biodegradable container. As you find litter, pick it up and put it into the container; dispose of it properly. (What kinds of things did you find on the beach? Make a chart to show how many of each you found.) Note: You may want to wear rubber gloves to protect yourself from any hazardous materials.

❏ Sea turtles are an endangered species. If you encounter one, be careful not to disturb it. Avoid its nesting grounds; sea turtles bury their eggs and you might accidentally crush them. Also, do not purchase any products made out of these animals. (On which beaches would you most likely see a sea turtle? What products are manufactured from them?)

❏ When you go boating, dispose of refuse properly. Dumping things off the boat and into the water can cause animals to become entangled in these objects. (List some things that are likely to cause entanglements. Explain what can happen if an animal becomes entangled in plastic 6-pack rings, etc.)

❏ If you buy helium-filled balloons, dispose of them properly. Balloons released into the air could possibly land in open waters where animals might swallow them. (Explain what could happen to a sea creature that swallowed a balloon. Find out if it is harmful to release helium into the atmosphere.)

❏ Write to either of the following agencies to find out more information about what you can do to help stop pollution on our beaches and waterways. Share any materials or information you receive with the class.

> ***Center for Marine Conservation***   ***The Oceanic Society***
> 1725 DeSales Street NW   218 D Street SE
> Washington, DC 20036   Washington, DC 20003

❏ Thousands of dolphins are captured and killed by tuna fisherman each year. (Find out what the tuna industry is currently doing about this problem. List some things you can do to help save the dolphins.)

Legends and Superstitions

A legend is a story handed down from generation to generation usually by oral retelling. Legends may explain something that happens in nature or convey a certain truth about life. Exaggeration plays an important role in the retelling of a legend.

The legend of the Manta Diablo is well known among the people of La Paz. Stories told by elders around fires at night reflect their encounters with the Manta Diablo. He is decribed as "larger than the largest ship in the harbor of La Paz. His eyes were the color of ambergris and shaped like a sickle moon and there were seven of them. He had seven rows of teeth in his mouth..."

Throughout our lives we hear about different legends such as Paul Bunyan, Pecos Bill, and Davy Crockett. Think about these legendary heroes and their incredible deeds. Then write about one of these legendary characters, or invent one of your own. Include exaggerated descriptions to make the character "larger than life." To prepare your thoughts, make a list of phrases that describe the character you will use in your legend. Por example, "Sam Southpaw had such a powerful swing that the crack of his bat could be heard around the world." Then use the phrases to develop a legend about your character..

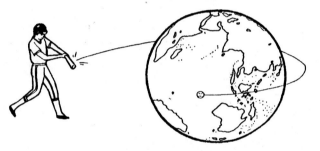

Some legends have their roots in superstition. Superstition is a belief that is inconsistent with known facts. It is based on fear of that which can not easily be explained.

Luzon is referred to in the story as a superstitious Indian. List some of his superstitions.

_____

_____

_____

_____

It is fun to learn about superstitions. Have you ever heard that if you break a mirror, you will have seven years of bad luck? List some superstitions you know or make up some of your own.

_____

_____

_____

Quiz Time!

1. On the back of this paper, write a one paragraph summary of the major events that happen in each of the chapters in this section. Then, complete the questions on the rest of this page.

2. Why does Ramon lie to his mother about what the weather is like?

   _____

   _____

3. Although Ramon has proven that he is a good diver, why is he still not allowed to sail with the fleet?

   _____

   _____

4. How does Luzon know the fleet has been lost?

   _____

   _____

5. Why does Sevillano return to the church?

   _____

   _____

6. Does Ramon believe that Luzon is telling the truth about the Manta Diablo? Do you believe Luzon?

   _____

   _____

7. What is Ramon planning to do with the pearl?

   _____

8. What did Ramon mean when he said Sevillano's voice was "hard"?

   _____

   _____

9. Why does Sevillano want Ramon to go with him to sell the pearl?

   _____

   _____

10. On the back of this paper, predict what Sevillano will do with Ramon after he has sold the pearl. Explain the reasons for your prediction.

Wanted!

The great pearl has been stolen! The people of La Paz are desperate to catch the culprit. You can help by designing a "wanted" poster. Be sure to list details about the stolen item and whom to contact if the pearl is found. Draw a picture in the box to accompany the details.

Figurative Language

Figurative language is often used in a story to help the author intensify an image. Examples include: "He is a *tiger* when he is angry" and "He eats *like a horse*." These statements are not meant to be taken literally. Rather, they are used to help the author better describe a subject or an action.

In small groups read the statements that follow. Then, determine what message the author is trying to give the reader by using figurative language. Be prepared to discuss your ideas.

1. (Ramon speaking of the Manta Diablo) "She told me that he was larger than the largest ship in the harbor of La Paz. His eyes were the color of ambergris and shaped like a sickle moon and there were seven of them. He had seven rows of teeth in his mouth, each tooth as long as my father's Toledo knife. With these teeth he would snap my bones like sticks." (page 7)

2. (Luzon speaking to Ramon) " 'It is well to hold the tongue and not to talk needlessly when you are on the lagoon. Remember this when we go out to dive, for there is one who listens and is quickly angered.' " (page 32)

3. (Luzon referring to the shell Ramon found) " 'In my life I have never seen such a monster. It is the grandfather of all oysters that live in the sea.' " (page 39)

4. (Ramon describing the pearl he found) "The great pearl caught the light, gathered it and softened it into a moon of dark fire . . .?" (page 53)

5. (Describing the big storm) "At midnight the wind still raged, but toward morning it slackened and at dawn died away in gasps, as a wounded beast dies." (page 64)

6. (Sevillano speaking to Ramon) " 'Do not think that I blame you for stealing the great pearl . . . For all the good it did it might better have been given to the devil.' " (page 73)

7. (Sevillano speaking to Ramon about the pearl) " 'You toss it to the devil and the devil picks it up.' " (page 74)

Stormy Weather

In chapter eleven of *The Black Pearl* there is a terrible storm. Ramon's mother predicts the storm because of changes that she notes in the weather. The wind, for instance, is hot and smells of the sea indicating that it is the chubasco (strong wind). Also, it is noted that there are no stars in the sky. Sure enough, as predicted, the dreadful storm materializes.

1. What changes in the weather have you noticed prior to a big storm?

   _____

   _____

   _____

2. What precautions do you take when you and your family find out that a big storm is headed for your town?

   _____

   _____

   _____

3. Does your school have an emergency plan for drastic weather conditions? If so, what is it? If not, what do you think the plan should include?

   _____

   _____

   _____

4. Find out the proper safety precautions you should take for a weather watch and a weather warning. What is the difference?

   _____

   _____

   _____

5. Find out what steps you should take when a storm threatens your electric service. Write them on the lines below.

   _____

   _____

   _____

Moral Dilemmas

Ramon faces some very difficult decisions in *The Black Pearl*. Some of his choices are good, others are not. Read the situations presented below. Respond to each by stating whether you think Ramon made a good decision or a poor one. Be sure to explain your answers.

1. Ramon is so upset about what happened to his father that he feels he has to return the pearl to the Manta Diablo before anything else happens. Consequently, he steals the pearl from the church. Do you think this is a good decision? What are Ramon's options? What would you do?

2. Ramon borrows a boat to sail to the lagoon. However, because he is in such a hurry, he does not ask the owner for permission to use the boat before leaving? Do you think this is a good decision? What are Ramon's options? What would you do?

3. When Sevillano asks Ramon for the pearl, Ramon throws it into the sea. Do you think this is a good decision? What are Ramon's options? What would you do?

Quiz Time!

1. On the back of this paper, write a one paragraph summary of the major events that happen in each of the chapters of this section. Then, complete the rest of the questions on this page.

2. How does Ramon know that the creature following them is the Manta Diablo?

_____

_____

3. Why is the island that Ramon and Sevillano are headed for called The Island of the Dead?.

_____

_____

4. Why don't the Indians want anyone on their island?

_____

_____

5. How is the great pearl responsible for the death of Ramon's father?

_____

_____

6. If Ramon has a knife, why doesn't he use it to try to get away from Sevillano?

_____

_____

7. What happens to Sevillano and the Manta Diablo?

_____

_____

8. Why do you think Ramon gives the pearl back to the church anonymously?

_____

_____

9. Why does Ramon feel that the day of his return to La Paz is the day "of his manhood"?

_____

_____

10. On the back of this paper, explain whether or not you think Sevillano got what he deserved.

Storyboard

A storyboard is similar to a comic strip. Notice the six blank areas in the storyboard below. Choose six main events that occurred in the chapters you have read in this section. Then, illustrate them in sequential order as they happened in the chapters. Finally, write a sentence describing the scene.

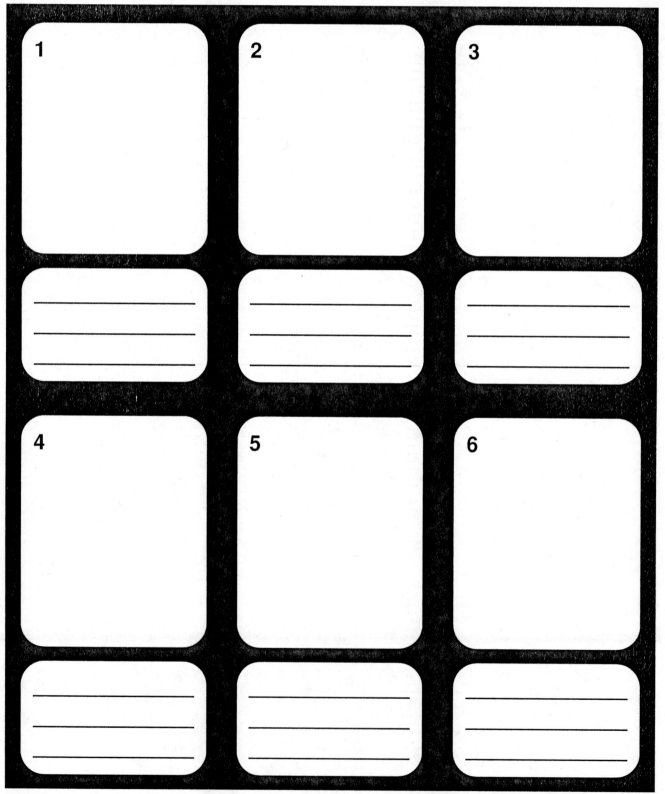

What If. . .?

Have you ever read a story and wished that it would have ended differently? Perhaps you even had an idea for a better ending. Sometimes, just by changing one event in a story the ending can be completely different.

Consider what may have happened in *The Black Pearl* if Sevillano hadn't been killed. In a small group, rewrite, in the space provided, the ending of the story with both Ramon and Sevillano still alive on the boat.

written by _____

_____

Marine Life Web

Although the Manta Diablo received most of the attention in *The Black Pearl,* he was certainly not alone in the vast ocean waters. The waters surrounding the Baja peninsula are teaming with marine life, some of which is represented in the pictures below.

In this activity, you will research one of the sea creatures from this page. Cut out the box containing your chosen topic and glue it in the center of the Marine Life Web on page 31. Write interesting facts on the rays of the web. Decorate the page further if you wish. Completed webs can be displayed in the classroom or compiled into a class reference book.

sea cucumber	eel	prawn	sea horse	abalone
sea otter	squid	sea urchin	penguin	shark
sponge	oyster	gull	coral	barnacles
octopus	crab	starfish	barracuda	seal
whale	lobster	sea turtle	jellyfish	dolphin

Marine Life Web *(cont.)*

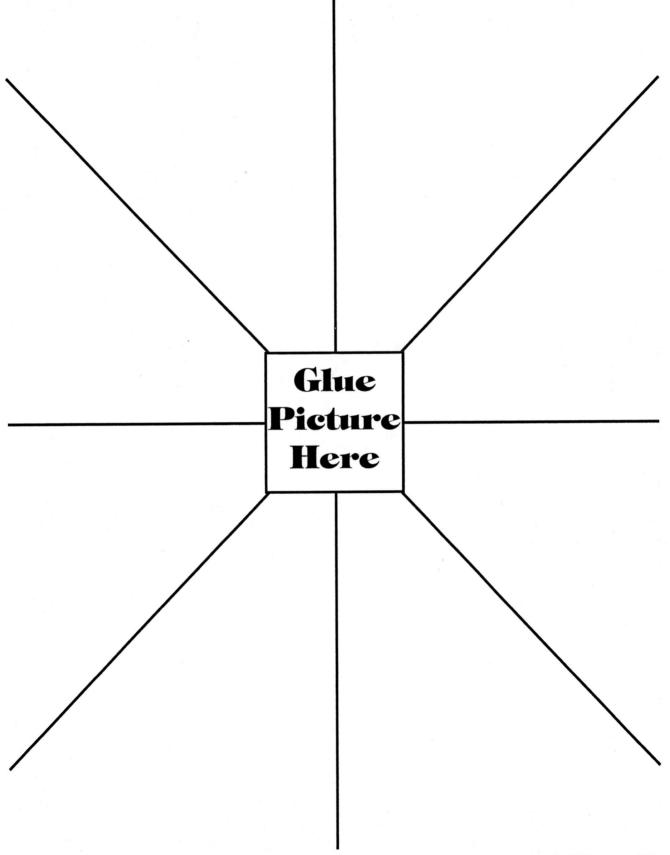

Crayon Resist Art Project

Draw a picture with your crayons of what you think Ramon may see when he goes diving. Fluorescent crayons work best, if you have them available. Be sure to draw plenty of fish and other sea life. Make it as colorful as possible. When you have finished drawing your picture, obtain a small cup of water and some blue and green watercolor paints. Mix the blue and green colors together, so you have a color similar to ocean water. Use this color to lightly paint over your entire picture. The crayon will resist the watercolor paint. Allow several hours to dry.

Missing Children

When Ramon leaves to return the pearl to the Manta Diablo, he does not tell his mother where he is going. Imagine the thoughts that go through her mind when Ramon and the pearl are both gone. Write a diary entry from Ramon's mother's point of view for the day she found out that Ramon was missing.

Date: _____ **Time:** _____

Take Time to Think. . .

Thousands of children are reported missing every year. It has become a nationwide problem. What precautions can parents take to help reduce the risk of their children being abducted? Write your ideas in the space provided.

What can you do? Think about your answers to the following questions. If necessary, discuss them with your parents. What are the family rules for answering the door or the phone when your parents are not home? What should you do if approached by a stranger? Compile your ideas and those of your classmates into a safety guide for younger children.

Word Search

```
f  l  a  w  f  r  s  d  i  s  g  u  s  t  g
o  b  m  a  l  i  c  e  g  t  r  s  d  i  b
v  e  s  e  d  a  y  j  i  r  u  h  e  l  a
e  t  i  c  g  y  g  b  n  e  n  r  s  l  r
r  r  e  a  o  r  l  o  a  w  t  e  p  e  r
c  a  l  r  e  f  g  n  o  n  m  w  e  r  e
a  y  d  a  s  l  f  r  t  n  g  d  r  n  n
s  g  d  t  n  e  u  e  m  o  h  t  a  f  l
t  a  u  t  e  b  r  t  d  i  m  i  t  m  p
n  x  h  d  c  b  l  s  p  t  o  j  i  a  r
p  e  m  a  n  h  o  o  d  r  n  i  o  e  o
u  z  c  k  i  c  n  h  a  c  o  e  n  l  s
n  i  c  h  e  a  g  p  r  o  w  n  s  g  p
y  e  r  t  a  d  o  r  a  t  i  o  n  e  e
d  s  a  d  m  o  n  i  t  i  o  n  i  s  r
```

Find and circle the following vocabulary words in the word search above:

flaw	puny	adoration	seize
disgust	grunt	resent	tiller
overcast	stern	strewn	taut
malice	niche	barren	desperation
scoff	admonition	betray	huddle
manhood	prow	shrewd	belfry
prosper	lagoon	timid	furlong
incense	gleam	carat	fathom

Teacher Note: See page 47 for answers.

Any Questions?

When you finished reading *The Black Pearl* did you have any questions that were left unanswered? Write them here.

_____

_____

_____

Work alone or in groups to prepare possible answers for the questions you asked above and those written below. When you have finished, share your ideas with the class.

- Will the church members find out who returned the pearl?
- Will Ramon continue to dive for pearls?
- What will happen to "Salazar and Son"?
- Is it possible that others in the fleet survived the storm?
- How might Ramon's life have been different if his father had returned home safely?
- With the Manta Diablo dead, will Luzon dive for pearls in the cave?
- What might happen if Ramon finds another great pearl?
- What will happen if the Manta Diablo is still alive?
- How will Ramon earn enough money to buy new boats to go diving?
- How will Mrs. Salazar help support the family?
- Will Ramon announce that he returned the pearl so he can collect a reward?
- What if the pearl had been lost during the struggle?
- Why doesn't Ramon have any friends?
- Why doesn't Ramon go to school?
- How is Ramon's life different from most 16 year olds in the United States?
- How would events have changed if Sevillano had lived?
- Will the church still display the pearl even though it had been stolen?
- Will Luzon and Ramon become business partners?
- Will Ramon confide in his mother about what really happened to him?
- Do you believe that manta diablos really exist?
- What will Ramon's life be like as an adult?
- Do people of other cultures or religions give gifts to their places of worship?

Book Report Ideas

There are numerous ways to report on a book once you have read it. After you have finished reading *The Black Pearl*, choose one method of reporting on the book that interests you. It may be a way that your teacher suggests, an idea of your own, or one of the ways that is mentioned below.

- **See What I Read?**

  This report is a visual one. A model of a scene from the story can be created, or a likeness of one or more of the characters from the story can be drawn or sculpted.

- **Come to Life!**

  This report is one that lends itself to a group project. A size-appropriate group prepares a scene from the story for dramatization, acts it out, and relates the significance of the scene to the entire book. Costumes and props will add to the dramatization.

- **Into the Future**

  This report predicts what might happen if *The Black Pearl* were to continue. It may take the form of a story in narrative or dramatic form, or a visual display.

- **A Letter to a Character**

  In this report, you may write a letter to any character in the story. You may ask him or her any questions that you wish. You may even want to offer some advice on a particular problem.

- **Guess Who or What**

  This report is similar to "Twenty Questions." The reporter gives a series of clues about a character or event in the story in a vague to precise, general to specific order. After all clues have been given, the character or event must be deduced. After the character has been guessed, the same reporter presents another twenty clues about an event in the story.

- **Ramon Returns!**

  Write a new story using Ramon as the main character. Other characters from *The Black Pearl* may also be used.

- **Coming Attraction!**

  The Black Pearl is about to be made into a movie, and you have been chosen to design the promotional poster. Include the title and author of the book, a listing of the main characters and the actors who will play them, a drawing of a scene from the book, and a paragraph synopsis of the story.

- **Book Review**

  Give an outline of the plot and then your opinion. Be sure to include both positive and negative points.

- **Literary Interview**

  This report is done in pairs. One student will pretend to be a character in the story, steeped completely in the persona of his or her character. The other student will play the role of a television or radio interviewer, trying to provide the audience with insights into the character's personality and life. It is the responsibility of the partners to create meaningful questions and appropriate responses.

Research Ideas

Describe three things that you read in *The Black Pearl* that you would like to learn more about.

1. _____

2. _____

3. _____

As you read *The Black Pearl,* you encountered geographical locations, scientific information, various legends, culturally diverse people, survival strategies, and a variety of sea creatures. To increase your understanding of characters and events in the story as well as recognize more fully Scott O'Dell's craft as a writer, research to find out more about these people, places, and things.

Work in groups to research one or more of the areas you named above, or the areas that are mentioned below. Share your findings with the rest of the class in an appropriate form of oral presentation.

Scuba Diving
equipment
techniques
professionals

Pearls
types
quality
value

Marine Biology
study
practice

Gems
pearls
rubies
sapphires
diamonds

Shellfish
oysters
clams

Oceanography
bathyscaph
Continental Drift
Naval Experimental Manned
Observatory

Cities in Mexico
Tijuana
La Paz
Guyamas
Guadalajara
Mexico City

Sea Creatures
sharks
eels
fish
stingrays

Sailing
how to
technical terms
famous vessels

Superstitions
causes of
cultural/traditional basis for

Legends
Paul Bunyan
Pecos Bill

Mexican Culture
history
religion
homes
language
customs and holidays

Diving For Treasure!

You have decided to learn to dive for pearls. On your first dive you find a black pearl even larger than the one Ramon found.

For this culminating activity, you will share your diving experience with the class. Here are some projects and writing ideas for you to complete.

- Create a cover sheet for your diving adventure.
- Briefly describe the moment that you found the great black pearl.
- List the qualities about you that made you such a good diver.
- Draw a picture of your boat.
- Explain why you decided to go diving that day.
- Express, in diary form, what was going through your mind as you sailed to where you would begin your dive.
- Describe what you did that morning to prepare for your dive.
- Describe how you opened the clam and felt for the pearl.
- Write, in a journal page, what went through your mind when you first laid eyes on the pearl.
- Describe your journey back to your home.
- Explain how you concealed the pearl on your way home.
- Describe the first person you will tell and what you will tell him/her about finding the pearl.
- Predict what you will ultimately do with your great pearl.
- What do your friends and family think you should do with the pearl? Write or tell about their opinions.
- Describe what happens once everyone in your town finds out that you found a great black pearl.
- Write about the reactions of those to whom you have told your story. Compare your story to Ramon's.
- Express your feelings about diving after your experience with the Manta Diablo.

Diving For Treasure! *(cont.)*

It is very important that you are prepared for any situation that could arise while on your diving trip. List below all the items you will need to take with you and the reasons why. Remember, you have a small boat which cannot carry an endless number of supplies, so choose carefully.

Item	Reason

Diving For Treasure! *(cont.)*

Your town is so pleased and proud of you for finding a great black pearl that they have decided to throw you a party. Design a flyer announcing the event. It might be fun to use a real picture of yourself in the flyer!

Diving For Treasure! *(cont.)*

With so many pearlers in your town, it is necessary to sail far away before finding an area that hasn't already been cleaned out. For your dive, you take an especially long trip to ensure that you will find waters in which no one has ever been diving before. Draw a map to show us the course you will take in reaching your destination.

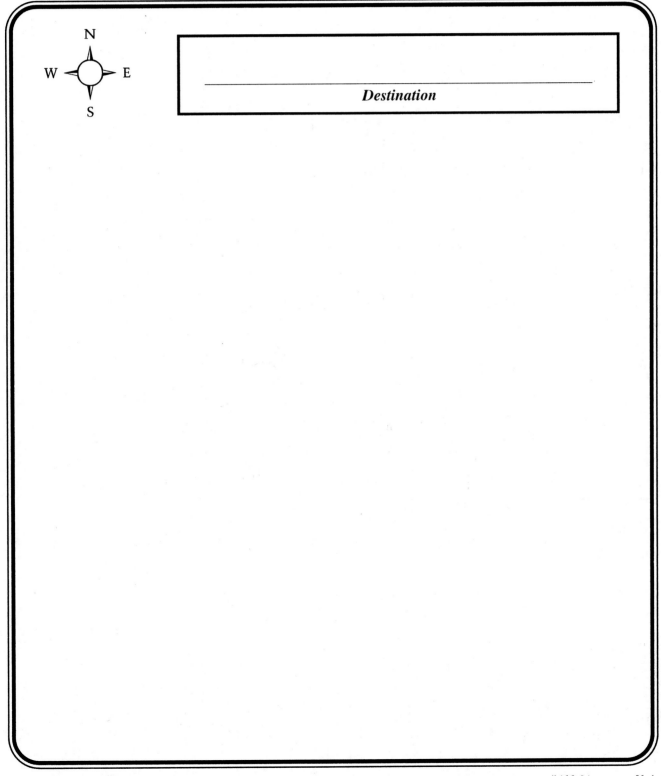

Unit Test

Matching: Match the Spanish word with its English meaning. Place the letter of the correct meaning on the line next to the matching Spanish word.

1. _____ *frijoles*   a. very strong wind
2. _____ *fiesta*   b. afternoon nap
3. _____ *coromuel*   c. jail
4. _____ *siesta*   d. light wind
5. _____ *chubasco*   e. beans
6. _____ *calabozo*   f. party

True or False: Write true or false next to each statement below.

1. _____ Ramon Salazar is 16-years-old.
2. _____ Sevillano is accidentally killed.
3. _____ Ramon's mother is a partner in the business.
4. _____ Ramon steals the pearl from the church.
5. _____ Ramon's mother is happy that they donated the pearl to the church.
6. _____ The pearl Ramon found weighs over 70 carats.

Short Answer: Write a short answer for each of these questions in the spaces provided.

1. What does the Manta Diablo look like?

_____

_____

2. Why does Sevillano get mad when Ramon tells him that the Manta Diablo is following them?

_____

_____

3. Why does Mr. Salazar give the pearl to the church rather than taking it to Mexico City to sell?

_____

_____

4. Why doesn't Luzon help Ramon pry open the huge shell Ramon has found?

_____

_____

Essay: Answer these questions on the back of this paper.

1. Describe the relationship between Ramon and Sevillano.
2. Describe how finding the great pearl changes Ramon's life.

Response

Explain the meaning of each of these quotations from *The Black Pearl*.

Chapter 1:   *"But before I speak about that time and the three of us there on the quiet sea in a struggle of death, before I tell what I know about the Manta Diablo, I must also tell about The Pearl of Heaven."*

Chapter 3:   *" 'About the Sevillano, let me repeat to you. Treat him with courtesy. Listen to his boasts as if you believed them. For he is a very dangerous young man.' "*

Chapter 6:   *" 'I cannot go to the cave to search for pearls. I cannot go because I fear the Manta Diablo. If you go there, then it is alone. El Diablo cannot blame me.' "*

Chapter 7:   *" 'And the big one you should throw there also . . . If you do not, señor, someday the Manta Diablo will have it back and your life with it. Of this I warn you.' "*

Chapter 8:   *" 'The flaw is gone. You have in your hand the Pearl of the Universe. The Paragon of Pearls. The great Pearl of Heaven.' "*

Chapter 9:   *" 'No, it was a gift from the House of Salazar. And for this gift of the great pearl, the greatest pearl ever found in the Vermilion Sea, the House of Salazar shall be favored in Heaven, now and forever.' "*

Chapter 10:   *" 'You are still a boy and there is much that you do not know. Therefore, I must tell you that the pearl does not belong to the Madonna nor to the church nor to the people who were singing. It belongs to the Manta Diablo and someday he will take it back. Of this I solemnly warn you.' "*

Chapter 11:   *" 'I have not seen the fleet . . . Nor will I ever see it again, nor will you, senor.' "*

Chapter 12:   *" 'The big Pearl of Heaven . . . did not bring us luck.' "*

Chapter 13:   *" 'Listen and let us be truthful. I know that you stole the big one. I stood at the door and saw you steal it and I also saw the bulge in your pocket when you came out from the church. Since we are truthful and you will wonder why I watched you I must say that I was there because I came to steal the pearl myself.' "*

Chapter 14:   *" 'I grow tired of our friend . . . If he swims closer I will give him a taste of the harpoon.' "*

Chapter 15:   *" 'I am aware that ignorant Indians believe in the Manta Diablo. But that you who have been to school and can read books, one of the mighty Salazars himself, should believe this fairy tale. Santa Rosalia, it surprises me!' "*

Chapter 18:   *" 'Outside, the sun now lay golden on the roof tops and the big bells were still ringing over the town. They rang in my heart, also, for this new day was the beginning day of my manhood.' "*

Teacher Note: Choose an appropriate number of quotations for your students.

Conversations

Work in groups to write and perform the conversations that might have occurred in the following situations.

- Ramon's mother is reprimanding him for something he did and she mentions the Manta Diablo. (2 people)

- Father Linares commands the Manta Diablo to return to the sea and remain there. (1 person)

- Ramon's mother and father discuss whether or not Ramon should be allowed to sail with the fleet. (2 people)

- The divers in the Salazar fleet begin preparations for a long trip. (4 or more people)

- A man tells Ramon's father about how Sevillano once killed a man. (2 people)

- Luzon tells his wife about the deal he has with Ramon to teach him how to dive. (2 people)

- Luzon tells the people of La Paz about Ramon's find and they all discuss it. (4 or more people)

- A man tells Sevillano about Ramon finding the great pearl. (2 people)

- A reporter interviews Ramon about the pearl. (2 people)

- The pearl dealers discuss what they will offer Mr. Salazar before they visit him. (3 people)

- Mr. and Mrs. Salazar discuss his decision to donate the pearl to the church. (2 people)

- Ramon's family is frightened of the storm. They voice their fears. (3 or more people)

- The storm destroys the fleet. Before going down the men try to help each other. (4 or more people)

- Father Gallardo tells the people of La Paz that the pearl has been stolen. (4 or more people)

- Ramon's mother realizes he has disappeared and calls the police. (2 people)

- Father Gallardo reports the stolen pearl to the police. (2 people)

- The detective considers the coincidence between the disappearance of Ramon and the pearl. (1 person)

- The Indians are angered when they see Sevillano and Ramon on their island. (4 or more people)

- Ramon tells his mother what happened between himself and Sevillano. (2 people)

- Ramon tells Father Gallardo that he returned the pearl. (2 people)

Bibliography

Anaya, Rudolph A. *Bless Me, Ultima.* (Tonatiuh-Quinto Sol International Publishing, 1972)

Batchelor, Julie Fosyth & De Lys, Claudia. *Superstitious? Here's Why.* (Scholastic Incorporated, 1954)

Brindze, Ruth. *All About Undersea Exploration.* (Random House, 1960)

dePaola, Tomie. *The Legend of the Indian Paintbrush.* (G.P. Putnam's Sons, 1988)

Dugan, James. *Undersea Explorer: The Story of Jacques Cousteau.* (Harper and Bros., 1957)

Floherty, John J. *Skin Diving Adventures.* (J.B. Lippincott Co., 1962)

Gardiner, John Reynolds. *Stone Fox.* (Thomas Y. Crowell, 1980)

Kipling, Rudyard. *Just So Stories.* (Penguin Books, 1987)

L'Engle, Madeleine. *Dragons in the Water.* (Dell Publishing, 1976)

McGovern, Ann. *Night Dive.* (Macmillan, 1984)

O'Dell, Scott. *Black Star, Bright Dawn.* (Ballantine Books, 1988)

      Carlota. (Dell Publishing, 1977)

      Castle in the Sea. (Ballantine Books, 1983)

      Island of the Blue Dolphins. (Dell Publishing, 1960)

      My Name is not Angelica. (Dell Publishing, 1989)

      The Serpent Never Sleeps. (Ballantine Books, 1987)

      Sing Down the Moon. (Dell Publishing, 1970)

      The Spanish Smile. (Ballantine Books, 1982)

      Streams to the River, River to the Sea. (Ballantine Books, 1986)

      Zia. (Dell Publishing, 1976)

Osborne, Mary Pope. *American Tall Tales.* (Alfred A. Knopf, 1991)

Rawls, Wilson. *Where the Red Fern Grows.* (Doubleday, 1984)

Sobol, Donald J. *True Sea Adventures.* (Thomas Nelson Inc., 1975)

Spinelli, Jerry. *Maniac Magee.* (Scholastic, 1990)

Ullman, James Ramsey. *Banner in the Sky.* (Scholastic, 1990)

Answer Key

Page 11

1. Accept appropriate responses.
2. Beauty describes its look and evil describes its personality.
3. If the fleet crashes, they would both die.
4. They might try to take advantage of Ramon.
5. Ramon, his father, an Indian and Sevillano were all sailing on the Santa Theresa.
6. Gaspar Ruiz is a braggart. He is tall, with wide shoulders, gold hair, blue eyes, and tattoos.
7. Ruiz is the best diver in La Paz.
8. Ramon is desperate to learn how to dive.
9. Ramon's dream is to find a great pearl.
10. Accept reasonable drawings.

Page 16

1. Accept appropriate responses.
2. When there is a red mist, the Manta Diablo is in the lagoon.
3. Ramon felt uncomfortable. He sensed danger.
4. Luzon is afraid of the Manta Diablo.
5. The pearl weighs 62.3 carats.
6. Ramon wants to tell his father about the pearl before anyone else does.
7. Luzon does not want any part of the pearl Ramon found in the lagoon.
8. They want the pearl to seem less valuable.
9. The family does not want to donate it.
10. Accept supported responses.

Page 19

Answers will vary depending on current exchange rates.

Page 22

1. Accept appropriate responses.
2. Ramon does not want his mother to worry.
3. Ramon's father wants him to run the office.
4. After surveying the damage, Luzon determined that no one could have survived the power of the storm.
5. Sevillano said he returned because he forgot his hat. But he really returned to steal the pearl.
6. Ramon now believes that Luzon has been telling the truth.
7. Ramon wants to return the pearl to the Manta Diablo.
8. His voice was stern and serious.
9. Sevillano can get more for the pearl if Ramon is with him.
10. Accept reasonable answers.

Page 24

Accept reasonable answers.

Page 26

Accept appropriate responses.

Page 27

1. Accept appropriate responses.
2. Ramon could tell by the way he looked that it was the Manta Diablo.
3. The island got its name because the Indians kill anyone that steps foot on the island.
4. The Indians are afraid their land will be taken away.
5. Ramon's father took a chance sailing since he thought he was protected because of his donation of the pearl to the church.
6. Ramon's knife is very dull.
7. Sevillano and the Manta Diablo die.
8. Accept reasonable, supported answers.
9. After all Ramon has been through, he considers himself an adult.
10. Accept appropriate responses.

Page 32

Create a bulletin board with these art projects.

Page 42

Matching
1) e   2) f   3) d   4) b   5) a   6) c

True or False
1. True   4. True
2. True   5. False
3. False   6. False

Short Answer
1. He is larger than the largest ship, seven eyes the color of ambergris that are sickle shaped. It has seven rows of teeth.
2. Sevillano becomes a little afraid that it could truly be the Manta Diablo. Until that moment he did not believe in its existence.
3. He had a bad experience in Mexico City the last time he was there.
4. Luzon is afraid that the Manta Diablo will think Luzon took the pearl if he helps Ramon.

Essay
1. Accept appropriate responses. Answers should reflect the animosity, rivalry, and jealously that existed between Ramon and Sevillano.
2. Accept appropriate responses. Included in the answer could be details about how Ramon began telling lies, his bad luck, and the death of his father.

Page 43

Accept all reasonable and well-supported answers.

Page 44

Perform the conversations in class. Ask students to respond to the conversations in several different ways, such as, "Are the conversations realistic?" or, "Are the words the characters use in keeping with their personalities?"

Answer Key *(cont.)*

Page 10 (Crossword Puzzle)

Page 34 (Word Search)

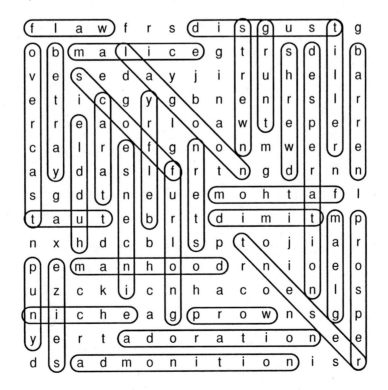

Pearl Pattern

See page 5 for suggested uses.